Helping Children See Jesus

ISBN: 978-1-64104-058-7

Christian Joy
New Testament Volume 30: Philippians

Author: Marilyn P. Habecker
Illustrator: Frances H. Hertzler
Computer Graphic Artist: Ed Olson
Typesetting and Layout: Patricia Pope

© 2018 Bible Visuals International
PO Box 153, Akron, PA 17501-0153
Phone: (717) 859-1131
www.biblevisuals.org

All rights reserved. No part of this publication may be reproduced, stored in a retrieval system or transmitted in any form by any means, electronic, mechanical, photocopy, recording or otherwise, without the prior permission of the publisher, except as provided by USA copyright law.

RELATED ITEMS

To access related items (such as activities, memory verse posters and translated texts) please visit our web store at www.biblevisuals.org and enter 1030 at the top right of the web page. You may need to reduce the zoom setting to get the search box.

FREE TEXT DOWNLOAD

To obtain a FREE printable copy of the English teaching text (PDF format) under Product Format, please scroll down and select Extra–PDF Teacher Text Download. Then under Language select English before clicking the ADD TO CART button to place in your shopping cart. Other languages are available at an additional cost from the Language menu. When checking out, use coupon code XTACSV17 at checkout and click on Apply Coupon to receive the discount on the English text.

Rejoice in the Lord alway: and again I say, Rejoice.

Philippians 4:4

© Bible Visuals International

Lesson 1
JOY IN SUFFERING (Christ the Master)

NOTE TO THE TEACHER

Although God's ways may seem mysterious, they are always best. The Apostle Paul found this to be so. He had a keen desire to go to Rome. He wanted to preach the Gospel there on the streets, or maybe even in the great Coliseum. He did get to Rome. However, instead of preaching to crowds, he preached to one's and two's in jail.

Those who visited him heard the Gospel. So did the soldiers who guarded him. In turn, they shared it with others so that some even in the palace received the Saviour. (See Philippians 4:22.)

For our sakes, it is good Paul had those years as a prisoner. During that time he wrote several New Testament books.

One of them, the book of Philippians, is the subject of our study in this series. The church at Philippi had sent gifts to Paul. (See Philippians 4:18.) In response, he wrote a thank you letter–the Philippian epistle. Philippians is filled with expressions of joy and rejoicing. (See, for example, 1:4, 18, 25, 26; 2:2, 16-18, 28; 3:1, 3; 4:1, 4, 10.)

Paul could have been disheartened since his own plans had been reversed. However, because Christ was his Master, his example, his prize, his strength, Paul had joy –fullness of joy. God wants you, teacher, and your pupils to experience this same joy.

Scripture to be studied: Philippians 1:1-30; Acts 16:12-40

The *aim* of the lesson: To show that it is possible for Christians to have joy, even in suffering.

What your students should *know*: They can have joy in suffering by trusting God completely. Because He is Master, His way is always best. (See Psalm 18:30; Philippians 2:13; Romans 8:28.)

What your students should *feel*: Gratitude for the joy God gives His own even in times of trial.

What your saved students should *do*: Determine to do something kind to the person who has caused them to suffer.

Lesson outline (For the teacher's and students' notebooks):

1. Suffering for doing good: Joy in the Philippian jail (Acts 16:10-40).
2. Suffering for testifying: Joy in a Roman jail (Philippians 1:12-18; Acts 24:11-15; 28:16-31).
3. Death does not mean suffering (Philippians 1:19-26).
4. Christians are appointed to suffer (Philippians 1:27-30).

The verse to be memorized:

Rejoice in the Lord alway: and again I say, Rejoice.
(Philippians 4:4)

THE LESSON

Let's start today by naming some things that make us happy. I would be happy if I had . . . (*Teacher:* Name something you would like to have.) What would make *you* happy?

(Let your class name a number of things. If possible, list them on a chalk board under the title *Happy*.)

The book which we begin studying today was written by the Apostle Paul when he had none of these things. His home was a prison. His companions were Roman soldiers to whom he was chained. There was the possibility of his being put to death at any time. (*Teacher:* Show that Paul had none of the items in the *Happy* list.) Even though he did not have that which makes us happy, Paul had joy. We may need things to make us happy. But we can have joy inside, even if we have nothing. For joy, like love and peace, comes from the Holy Spirit. (See Galatians 5:22-23.)

The Philippians were delighted when Paul's letter came. Who do you suppose was present when it was read? What were their thoughts? What did they say? We do not know, but it may have been like this: The whole assembly smiled when they heard the words: "I thank God every time I remember you who are in Philippi. I pray for you with joy, remembering how we worked together in the Gospel from the first day until now." (See Philippians 1:4-5.)

That pleased all the Philippians. About ten years had passed since Paul was in their city. Much had happened since then. Still Paul had joy when he prayed for them, remembering his Gospel work with them.

Show Illustration #1A

It was Lydia who caught the words, "from the first day." When Paul first came to Philippi, he preached the Gospel to her and other women at the riverside. The Lord opened her heart that day. Then she opened her home to Paul and his missionary companions–Silas, Timothy, Luke. (See Acts 16:15, 40.) Having them in her home was her way of working together with them in the Gospel "from the first day." Lydia felt certain that Paul remembered her. She smiled contentedly.

Show Illustration #1B

Sitting near Lydia was another woman who listened earnestly to Paul's letter. She was but a young girl when Paul had been in Philippi. A demon had control of her then. It made her able to tell what was going to happen in the future. The men who owned her made a lot of money from her fortune telling. For days she followed Paul and the other missionaries, shouting loudly. Finally Paul spoke sharply to the demon saying, "I command you in the name of Jesus Christ to come out of her." Immediately the Lord Jesus set her free and changed her life completely.

Had Paul been thinking of her when he wrote, "God who began a good work in you will continue working in you until Jesus Christ comes again"? (See Philippians 1:6.) She, who was once owned by wicked men and controlled by a demon, now belonged to the Lord Jesus Christ. She was encouraged to know that He would continue His good work in her.

1. SUFFERING FOR DOING GOOD (JOY IN THE PHILIPPIAN JAIL)
Acts 16:10-40

A strong, rigid man was doubtless among those who heard Paul's letter. His face showed the marks of a hard life. He was the jailer at Philippi, a man used to handling criminals. Ten years before, some men had dragged Paul and Silas to his prison. They were charged with speaking against the law of the land. (See Acts 16:20-21.) The truth was that the missionaries had dismissed a demon from a young girl. They had done so by the power of Jesus Christ. So the men who owned her were angry and threw Paul and Silas into prison. The jailer could still remember how securely he had fastened them in the inside jail.

Show Illustration #1C

He had never seen such strange prisoners as Paul and Silas. They did not protest. They did not swear. They were not angry. They were full of joy–so joyful that they sang hymns at midnight! And finally, when an earthquake opened the prison doors and unfastened their chains, they did not try to escape. They remained there and told the jailer the way of salvation. Consequently, he, his family, and his servants believed in the Lord Jesus and were baptized that same night.

Now, years later, it was as if Paul was writing to him alone. For the letter continued, "You are dear to me. While I was in prison . . . we shared together God's loving favor." (See Philippians 1:7.)

Paul had suffered for doing good to a demon-possessed girl. However, since Christ was Master of his life, Paul experienced joy in suffering.

2. SUFFERING FOR TESTIFYING
(JOY IN A ROMAN JAIL)
Philippians 1:12-18; Acts 24:11-15; 28:16-31

From the time Paul first visited their city, the Philippians were concerned for him. (See Philippians 4:15-16.) His missionary journeys had taken him to many places. Everywhere he testified that his trust was in the Lord Jesus Christ who died and rose again. Because of his testimony in Jerusalem (See Acts 21:27–24:27.), Paul spent two years in prison in Caesarea. Even when the officials had him on trial, Paul testified that Jesus died and rose from the grave. (See Acts 25:19; 26:23.) Because of his testimony, Paul was now in jail in Rome. God could have opened the prison doors as He had done in Philippi, but He did not. The Philippians wondered how Paul was enduring his punishment. Was he discouraged? Did he want them to do something to get him released? They listened attentively to his letter.

Show Illustration #2

"I want you to know, Christian brothers," he said, "that everything that has happened to me has helped to spread the Gospel of Christ. All the soldiers know I am here because I am a Christian." (See Philippians 1:12-13.)

Every few hours another soldier was brought in and chained to the Apostle Paul. He was their most unusual prisoner. He did not curse. He was not angry at the authorities who put him in jail. Instead, he talked about his Saviour, the Son of God. He told how he had been completely changed when he trusted in Jesus Christ. Since these soldiers were the special group who guarded the emperor, they repeated the Gospel message in the palace. (See Philippians 1:12-13.)

There were others in Rome who were hearing the Gospel. Paul explained why that was so: "Many Christians here in Rome have seen me in chains. Somehow this has encouraged them. They have become much more bold and are not afraid to testify. There are some who are jealous of the way God has used me. But they, too, are out preaching. [*Teacher:* Point to top right of illustration.] So the Gospel of Christ is being told, and I am rejoicing and will continue to rejoice." (See Philippians 1:14-18.)

The reading of the letter was interrupted. The Philippians all talked at once. "Even in jail he is rejoicing!" "He's not even concerned that some are preaching because they're jealous of him!" "The only thing Paul wants is to have the Gospel made known!" "No one can kill that man's joy!"

3. DEATH DOES NOT MEAN SUFFERING
Philippians 1:19-26

Again the reader must have picked up Paul's letter and continued reading. "I hope I shall never be ashamed, but that I'll be bold in witnessing." (See Philippians 1:20.) The Philippians understood. Guards were rough, crude and powerful. It was not easy for a prisoner to break into their dirty talk and introduce them to the Saviour. They would ridicule him, perhaps punish him. For this reason Paul added, "I want others to see how wonderful Christ is, whether I live or whether I die. If I stay here on earth, I can lead more people to Christ . . . but to be in Heaven with Christ is far better." (See Philippians 1:21-23.)

Show Illustration #3

The Philippians considered this. They were aware that Paul suffered as a prisoner. They thought that if he died, he would suffer even more. According to Paul just the opposite was true. To die is to gain something far better than life. Death means being in God's home, free from all suffering forever.

4. CHRISTIANS ARE APPOINTED TO SUFFER
Philippians 1:27-30

After mentioning that the Philippians had the privilege of trusting in Christ, he added this warning: "You must also suffer for Him." (See Philippians 1:29.)

So they, too, would have to suffer! Paul was a great missionary and a great preacher. He knew God so well that he could go through suffering. But what would happen to them, especially if they each had to suffer alone?

If Paul could have answered the Philippians' questions, he would have told them of his own experiences:

Show Illustration #4A

"During our second missionary journey, I was dreadfully discouraged. The officials in one city after another had forced us to leave. (See Acts 16:39; 17:10, 13-14, 32-33.) When I was wondering how to proceed, the Lord spoke to me at night in a vision. He said, 'Do not be afraid, but speak . . . for I am with you.' " (See Acts 18:9-10.)

"On another occasion I was on trial. It ended in an uproar. I would have been killed, except that the captain rescued me and kept me in the castle overnight." (See Acts 23:1-11.)

Show Illustration #4B

"That night the Lord stood by me, saying, 'Be of good cheer, Paul. As you have testified of me in Jerusalem, so you must witness also in Rome.'

"While sailing to Rome, we got in a raging storm. Everyone expected that the ship and all the passengers would be lost.

Show Illustration #4c

"One night, when things seemed their worst, an angel of God stood by me. He said, 'Do not be afraid, Paul. You and all who sail with you will be safe.' " (See Acts 27:1-44.)

The One who was always with Paul has promised that He will never leave *you*, nor forsake *you*. Because that is so, you may boldly say, "The Lord is my helper, and I will not fear what man shall do to me." (See Hebrews 13:5-6.) He will be with you, even in suffering, giving you His joy. (See John 15:11.)

Perhaps you are having some trial right now. Someone may have ridiculed you for doing good. Or maybe you have been laughed at for testifying about the Lord Jesus. It could be that somebody has made fun of you because you are a Christian. Your experience may be unpleasant. But if Christ is your Master, you can have joy because you know He is in control of everything. His joy will lead you to do something kind for the one who has been unkind to you. Write in your notebook the name of the person who has caused you to suffer. Decide what kind thing you could do for him (her). Write that in your notebook. Then we shall pray that God will help you to do that kindness this week.

Lesson 2
JOY IN HUMILITY (Christ, the Believer's Example)

NOTE TO THE TEACHER

In Philippians 2, Christ is presented as the believer's perfect example of humility. Here Christ's voluntary emptying of Himself is expressed in four ways:

1. He took the form of a servant. Christ chose to serve men although He is God.
2. He was made in the likeness of men. He had a body. That body had the same physical needs as our bodies.
3. He was found in fashion as a man. He wore similar clothing and looked the same as other men of His day.
4. He became obedient to death. He chose to suffer the humiliating death of crucifixion even though He had the power to save Himself from it.

Christ has set the perfect example of humility for us who are believers. Depending upon the needs of your group, you may want to mention how Paul emphasized humility in his epistles. (See Romans 12:3; 1 Corinthians 1:10-29; 2 Corinthians 12:7; Galatians 5:26; Ephesians 4:1-2; Colossians 3:12; 1 Timothy 6:11.) The first requirement of walking worthy of the Lord is to walk humbly with all lowliness and meekness. Pray that you will be a humble servant, teacher. It is good to be an able teacher. To be a humble teacher is better.

Since the last lesson some of your students may have done something kind for someone who had caused them to suffer. Give them opportunity to tell the results of their kind deeds.

Scripture to be studied: Philippians 2

The *aim* of the lesson: To show that the Lord Jesus is the perfect example of humility.

What your students should *know*: That those who are truly humble will have joy.

What your students should *feel*: A keen desire to humble themselves.

What your saved students should *do*: Humble themselves, first. Then go to anyone with whom they have argued and seek to settle the disagreement.

Lesson outline (For the teacher's and students' notebooks):

1. Believers are to be humble (Philippians 2:1-4).
2. Christ, our Example, humbled Himself (Philippians 2:5-11).
3. Humble believers are to be lights (Philippians 2:12-16).
4. Examples of humility (Philippians 2:17-300).

The verse to be memorized:

Rejoice in the Lord alway: and again I say, Rejoice.
(Philippians 4:4)

THE LESSON

Have you ever had a nasty quarrel with another Christian? How did you feel afterwards when you had to be near that person? If (s)he sat alongside you right now, what would you do?

1. BELIEVERS ARE TO BE HUMBLE
Philippians 2:1-4

Many of the Philippian Christians probaby sat quietly enjoying the reading of Paul's letter.

However, there were some unhappy ones who squirmed from time to time. Unfortunately, two ladies in the Philippian church had had a severe quarrel. (See Philippians 4:2.)

Show Illustration #5

As a result, some of the church members had taken sides. Neither group had any joy, and their bad feelings showed on their faces. They purposely ignored each other. Word of the division had reached Paul hundreds of miles away in Rome.

Early in his letter Paul told them, "You *all* . . . are dear to me." (See Philippians 1:7.) Those on opposing sides were annoyed. They wondered how Paul could say that those on the other side were dear to him.

Paul added, "Stand fast in one spirit. With one mind strive together . . . . Make my joy full by agreeing with each other. Love each other. Be one in your thoughts and actions." (See Philippians 1:27; 2:2.) So! Paul could have full joy if they would agree and love each other. The Philippians squirmed. "Do not quarrel. Do not have too high an opinion of yourself," Paul continued. "Be humble. Think of others as more important than yourself." (See Philippians 2:3.)

Both groups were embarrassed. They expected Paul to be concerned about his own suffering in prison. Instead, he was concerned for them! He had not come right out and said they were proud. But what else could he mean when he urged them to be humble? They were ashamed.

2. CHRIST, OUR EXAMPLE, HUMBLED HIMSELF
Philippians 2:5-11

To help them, Paul explained what they should do. "You must follow the example of Christ Jesus," he said. (See Philippians 2:5.)

Show Illustration #6
Jesus Christ was always with God, Paul explained. He (with God the Father and God the Holy Spirit) created everything. (See John 1:1-3; Colossians 1:16; Hebrews 1:1-8; compare Genesis 1:2; Psalm 102:24-25; 104:30; Job 26:13.) The Lord Jesus had all the qualities of God and was equal with Him, but He put on the form of a servant. He, the Creator, left the ivory palaces of heaven. (See Psalm 45:8.) He laid aside His own glory, His own reputation, His own will and His own comforts. He came down to earth, as a helpless baby with only a manger for a bed. He who was worshiped by angels became a servant. (See Hebrews 1:6; Matthew 20:28; Mark 10:45; John 13:2-17.)

Paul continued his explanation: The Lord Jesus Christ, who was one with God, stooped to become a man. Then He humbled Himself even further: He willingly gave Himself to die a shameful death on a cross. (Compare Hebrews 12:2.)

Because Christ humbled Himself, God has raised Him high above everything else. He has given Him a name that is greater than all others. A day will come when everyone will bow down before Him. Each shall declare openly that Jesus Christ is the Lord, to the glory of God the Father. (Even the devil and his angels will bow! See Philippians 2:6-11.)

The quarrelsome, unhappy Philippians must have been downcast. Would they follow the example of the Lord Jesus and humble themselves as Paul suggested?

3. HUMBLE BELIEVERS ARE TO BE LIGHTS
Philippians 2:12-16

Because Christ humbled Himself, God highly exalted Him. (*Teacher*: The "therefore" of verse 12 refers to what precedes in verses 8-11.) So Paul added this advice: "Therefore, work out the solution to your own difficulty [which is the meaning of the word *salvation* in this instance]–Even though I am not there, you yourselves can work this out." (See Philippians 2:12.) That is, if you will be willing to follow the example of Christ and humble yourself; if you will give up your desire for your reputation, your honor; if you will think as Christ thought, you can work out your problem. God exalted the Lord Jesus because He humbled Himself. And God will bless you if you humble yourselves. "Work out the solution to your argument. Be afraid of displeasing God. He is in you and will help you to do what will please Him having agreement in your church."

[See Philippians 2:13.] Do everything without grumbling and arguing, so you will be without blame." (See Philippians 2:14.) That command struck hard. Many who had not taken sides in the argument had doubtless grumbled about the whole affair. Now most of the Philippians were uneasy.

"You are children of God," Paul reminded them. People should be able to tell that you belong to God by the way you live. Show that you are like Him. "You live in a dark, sinful world. Shine as lights!" (See Philippians 2:15; Matthew 5:16.)

Show Illustration #7A
The Philippians may have glanced around the congregation. There were some who were letting their lights shine. They were always doing good things for others. Consequently, they didn't have time to grumble or take part in the argument. Their faces showed their joy. The others looked dismal. No one could see any light in them. What a disgrace!

Show Illustration #7B
"You have the Word of God which gives life. Share it with others so that they will have life–eternal life. If you shine as lights and tell out the Word of life, I shall be able to rejoice when I stand before Christ. For then I will know that my work among you was worthwhile." (See Philippians 2:16.)

The Philippians were amazed that what they did affected Paul's joy. Earlier he had told them that they could make his joy full right now even in jail by agreeing and loving each other. (See Philippians 2:2.) Here he was saying that if they shine as lights (instead of arguing) and proclaim the Word of life, they will rejoice when they stand before Christ.

4. EXAMPLES OF HUMILITY
Philippians 2:17-30

Show Illustration #8A
Paul had more to say. "Those who are holding me prisoner may put me to death. You have sacrificed and served the Lord because of your faith in Him. If I can add to your service by giving my life, it will be joy for me. You, too, must have joy and rejoice with me." (See Philippians 2:17-18.)

This was almost too much for the Philippians. They remembered how harshly Paul had been treated when he brought the Gospel to their city. (See Acts 16:12-40; 1 Thessalonians 2:2.) This he never mentioned.

He spoke only of their work for the Lord. It was their work– not his in which he was interested. It was their sacrifice–not his–that gave him joy. The Philippians realized that they did not have Paul's kind of humility.

"If the Lord is willing, I want to send Timothy to see you, Paul declared. "Then he can come back and cheer me with news from you. He is genuinely concerned about you. You know how he has proved himself in the work of the Gospel. He has been like a son with a father" (Philippians 2:19-22).

Show Illustration #8B
The Philippians nodded. They admired Timothy. He had worked as hard as Paul when they had been in Philippi together. Lydia recalled their coming to the riverside to preach. Now, ten years later, Timothy was still standing by Paul. He could be a fine pastor of some church. He chose instead to help

the aging prisoner, Paul. Did the Philippians have that kind of humility?

"I am sending Epaphroditus to you," Paul wrote.

At the mention of Epaphroditus, the Philippians came to attention. He was the messenger who had taken their gifts to Paul. (See Philippians 4:18.) In the meantime, word had reached them that Epaphroditus was seriously ill. Everyone was concerned about him.

Show Illustration #8C

Paul proceeded: "Epaphroditus, my brother (in Christ), has been homesick for you and was worried because you heard he was sick. He almost died while working for Christ. He was doing things for me that you could not do. [See Philippians 2:25-30.] Welcome him in the Lord with joy. Hold him in high honor."

The Philippians got the message. Although Epaphroditus had suffered a great deal because of taking their gift to Paul, he was not concerned about that. What did trouble him was that they had learned of his sickness. He was sorry about that. He did not want them to be worried–not for a moment. Only a truly humble man would feel like that.

The Philippians had to make some decisions after listening to Paul's letter. They may have thought about the quarrel between the two women and how various ones had taken sides. Surely they would want to humble themselves and apologize. And you, too, must make some decisions. Have you had an argument with another Christian? Are you willing to admit that the other person could be right? Will you follow the example of the Lord Jesus Christ who humbled Himself? Will you go to the other person and settle the argument? Write the name of the person in your notebook. Let's pray together that you will humble yourself. Then we shall ask God to show you what to say so the disagreement can be corrected. After that you will be a light, shining for Christ.

Lesson 3
JOY IN SACRIFICE (Christ, the Prize)

NOTE TO THE TEACHER

Philippians is the epistle of joy. Circumstances may be exactly opposite from that which makes for peace or gladness. Yet the one whose trust is in the Lord can always look above the circumstances. Christ is over all. There are no second causes with Him. All that comes to the Christian is permitted by Him.

It is the Christian's privilege and duty to rejoice in the Lord. Holiness and happiness are tied together. If you are walking close to the Lord, your joy will be evident. His joy will be your strength. (See Nehemiah 8:10.) Your students will be challenged if you are a strong, joyous Christian–especially if you have made sacrifices for Christ's sake.

Give your students opportunity to tell of experiences they had in working out last week's lesson. Were they able to settle their arguments with other Christians? What were the reactions of their friends?

Scripture to be studied: Philippians 3

The *aim* of the lesson: To show that even when we are called upon to make sacrifices for Christ's sake, He blesses us with His joy.

What your students should *know*: That Paul, probably the greatest of missionaries, gave up everything for Christ.

What your students should *feel*: A desire to have the joy of the Lord, no matter what sacrifice is necessary.

What your students should *do*: If position, or possessions, or achievements, or liberty are of more importance than Christ, be willing to sacrifice it (or them) right now.

Lesson outline (for the teacher's and students' notebooks):

1. Sacrificing position (Philippians 3:1-7).
2. Sacrificing possessions (Philippians 3:8-9).
3. Sacrificing past achievements (Philippians 3:10-14).
4. Sacrificing liberty (Philippians 3:15-21).

The verse to be memorized:

Rejoice in the Lord alway: and again I say, Rejoice.
(Philippians 4:4)

THE LESSON

Have you ever taken part in a race? Was it fun? Was it easy? (Allow time for answers.) Was a prize given to the winner of the race?

You have all heard of the Olympic games. These were begun hundreds of years ago in ancient Greece. In those early years the victor's prize was a crown of wild olive leaves–leaves that soon withered. Today the first prize is a gold medal.

The person who takes part in the Olympics must have disciplined training. If he is a runner, he runs day after day. When night comes his legs ache, his chest hurts, his feet stumble. He is too exhausted to spend time with his friends. Week after week and month after month he runs and runs and runs, desperately hoping to set a new record.

Finally the day of the race comes. Off he goes! He does not turn to smile at the cheering crowd. He does not stop to get a drink of water. He does not look back to see the other runners. He keeps his eyes on the goal. As he pushes himself harder than he thought possible, his chest feeling as if it may burst, his head pounding, he forges ahead and wins the race. Later he stands before the spectators and receives a medal. Months, perhaps years of sweat and strain–all for the sake of a medal. Does he think of the sacrifices of going without certain foods, practicing when he could have been playing, falling into bed too exhausted to be with his friends? He does not. He's happy. He won the prize. That is all that matters.

Paul doubtless had the Olympics in mind when he wrote his letter to the Philippians. He thought of the Christian life as a race. In chapter three he speaks of the Christian's prize. Since we do not know what the Philippians thought when they heard his letter, we shall have to use our imaginations.

1. SACRIFICING POSITION
Philippians 3:1-7

Everyone grinned and exchanged glances upon hearing, "Rejoice in the Lord! I do not mind repeating this advice. It is good for you." (See Philippians 3:1.)

One man whispered to another, "It's easy to rejoice sitting here with other Christians. I wonder how Paul can do it with those rough guards in prison."

Paul continued: "Beware of dogs, those evil workers who try to get you to follow Jewish ceremonies. They think you must go through the religious act of becoming a Jew in order to be a Christian. That ritual has nothing to do with salvation. We dare not depend upon good things we do, not even religious ceremonies. God does not accept people because of their high position or because they have done good things. Let me tell you, I had more to put me in favor with God than most people have. I was a Jewish leader. Listen to this:

Show Illustration #9A

1. "I had the Jewish RITE [of circumcision] when I was eight days old.
2. "I was born in the Jewish RACE. I belonged to one of the best tribes, the tribe of Benjamin. Jews, you know, are God's own special people.
3. "I could boast of my RELIGION. I belonged to the Pharisees, the strictest of all the Jewish religious groups. I knew and obeyed every law and command of the Jewish religion.
4. "I had a magnificent RECORD in my work. Since I was a Jew I believed Christians were blasphemers because they worshiped Jesus. So I broke into homes and tore men and women away from their families and dragged them to prison. [See Acts 8:1-3; 9:1-2.] I really thought I was pleasing God by making it hard for Christians.
5. "I was RIGHTEOUS. No one could find fault with me. Why? Because I kept the Jewish law; I obeyed every command; I offered every sacrifice; I observed every feast day."

(*Teacher*: Your pupils should write in their notebooks what Paul said about himself. See above. Reference: Philippians 3:5-6.)

The Philippians nodded in agreement. Everything Paul had said was true.

Show Illustration #9B

"My position as a Jewish leader was most important to me," Paul continued. "Then I met Christ, and all was changed. I turned my back on the things I valued and gave them up for Him." (See Philippians 3:7.)

2. SACRIFICING POSSESSIONS
Philippians 3:8-9

"Now I am much older. I have suffered a great deal. All that I had is gone." The Philippians knew the truth of that. Paul was in prison as he wrote, but this was one of many imprisonments. He had been lashed and beaten. Once he was stoned and left for dead. He had been shipwrecked. There were times when he was in pain, hungry, thirsty, cold, and without clothes. (See 2 Corinthians 11:23-27.) The congregation shook their heads sympathetically, remembering what he had suffered for Christ's sake. Paul, the man with the fine education, the great preacher, the energetic missionary, now had nothing. They wondered how he felt about losing everything.

Show Illustration #10A

The next line of his letter told them. "All those things that I was and what I had are worthless rubbish compared with Christ." (Compare Isaiah 64:6.)

"Before I was a Christian, I did things to try to get in right standing with God. But I never succeeded."

Show Illustration #10B

"Now I am in right standing with God, but only because of what the Lord Jesus has done. [See Hebrews 10:14.] When I placed my trust in Him, God declared me righteous. To know that I have perfect standing before God is greater far than all the good things I had before I was saved."

3. SACRIFICING PAST ACHIEVEMENTS
Philippians 3:10-14

"That does not mean that I am perfect. Far from it!" (See 1 Corinthians 9:27.)

The Philippians understood what Paul meant. His salvation was perfect; that is, it was complete. Nothing could be added to or taken away from his salvation. But they realized that Paul (like every Christian) still had his old sinful nature. He sinned after he was saved and had to ask forgiveness for those sins. But God never takes away the gift of salvation. Salvation is perfect. It cannot be changed. Saved people, however, are not perfect. They need to be changing, growing constantly.

Paul continued, "I think of the Christian life as a race. The goal is to be a full-grown Christian. I should be making progress, just as a runner progresses in a race. I should know the will of God for each new day. [See Colossians 4:12.] I should be set apart [holy] for God every day [2 Corinthians 7:1]. I should be patient in every circumstance [James 1:4]. I should continually do good work for God [Hebrews 13:21]. I want to keep advancing in the race of life. This keeps me so busy that I am forgetting completely the things that are behind."

The Philippians all talked at once. "How can he do that? Anyone who has done as much good as he has, should not forget it! Think of all the people he has won to Christ. He even had converts in Athens right in the shadow of the idols! Why should he forget that?" They listened to hear what was next.

Show Illustration #11

"I am stretching forward, reaching for the goal. The race will soon be over, and I will have the prize." What prize could be greater than to be like Christ [1 John 3:2], and to be with Him forever? How can I help but rejoice?"

4. SACRIFICING LIBERTY
Philippians 3:15-21

Show Illustration #12A

"Now, if you are growing spiritually day by day, if you are straining forward toward the goal, you must get along with each other. Settle the argument you have had. We are all in this race together." (See Philippians 3:15-16.) Once again the Philippians were embarrassed. "God will show you His will, which might prove that both sides are wrong. By nature, we all want our own way. Choose God's way instead.

"Christian brothers, I want all of you together to follow me. Imitate my life. I have given you an example of how a Christian should live." The Philippians needed that advice. They had no New Testament to guide them, as we have today. Paul's life was a good pattern.

"Let me warn you of something," Paul added. "I am crying when I tell you this. There are many who want you to follow them. I have told you about them before. They say they love God. Some say they have faith in Christ. However, they do not believe it is necessary to live holy lives. They think it is all right for people to sin. They make a god out of their stomachs. They take pride in things they should be ashamed of. All they think about are the things of this world. As far as they are concerned, Christians can live any way they want to. I tell you, they are the enemies of Christ. God will destroy them."

When we become Christians, we give up our liberty to live as we please. Paul continues, "Remember this: we are citizens of Heaven." Heaven is our home. That is where we belong. What a beautiful place! Bright, so bright that no sun is needed there. No one has pain or suffering in Heaven. No one dies in Heaven. God is there; the Lord Jesus is there. Some day we will be there. Until then, let us live pure lives, just as if we were already in God's presence. When we live to please Him, He gives us joy.

Show Illustration #12b

One of these days, the Lord Jesus will come in the clouds. In a moment, He will change believers' weak bodies, making them like His. Together we shall go up with Him, to be with Him forever. (See Philippians 3:20-21; 1 Corinthians 15:51-52; 1 Thessalonians 4:13-18.) He is coming again. We will go up with Him. That's enough to make any Christian rejoice!

Paul sacrificed everything. He gave up his position as a Jewish leader. He let go of all that he had. He refused to think of the things he had accomplished. He did not live as he pleased. He sacrificed everything so he could become a full-grown Christian. Consequently, God gave him joy–fullness of joy.

If you do not have Christian joy, if you cannot rejoice, perhaps it is because something is more important to you than the Lord Jesus. You have never been willing to sacrifice that thing. Whatever it is, will you tell the Lord about it? If He wants you to give it up, will you do that right now? (*Teacher:* Allow quiet time for students to make decisions.)

Lesson 4
JOY IN SURRENDER (Christ, the Believer's Strength)

NOTE TO THE TEACHER

The theme of the fourth chapter of Philippians is *Joy in Surrender*. It is Christ who gives the believer strength to surrender to His will. (See Philippians 4:13.) Those who surrender their rights receive the peace of God. (See 4:7.) Those who surrender their thoughts have the God of peace with them. (See 4:9.) God gives contentment to those who surrender their wills to Him. (See 4:11.) Christians who surrender their money have this promise: "My God shall supply all your need according to His riches in glory by Christ Jesus." (See 4:19.) May your own life, teacher, be an example in these matters.

Give your students opportunity to tell of the joy the Lord has given them since they sacrificed something which had been more important than Christ.

Scripture to be studied: Philippians 4

The *aim* of the lesson: To show that God has specific blessings for those who surrender their rights, their thoughts, their wills, their money to Him.

What your students should *know*: That Christ will give them strength to do whatever God asks them to do.

What your students should *feel*: A yearning for all the blessings and joy God wants them to have.

What your students should *do*: Surrender to the Lord.

Lesson outline (for the teacher's and students' notebooks):
1. Surrendering our rights (Philippians 4:1-7).
2. Surrendering our thoughts (Philippians 4:8-9).
3. Surrendering our wills (Philippians 4:10-13).
4. Surrendering our money (Philippians 4:14-23).

The verse to be memorized:

Rejoice in the Lord alway: and again I say, Rejoice.
(Philippians 4:4)

THE LESSON

In a war, both armies want to win. The fighting is fierce and rough. No matter how hard it is to fight, to surrender is even harder. Neither army likes to surrender.

In closing his letter to the Philippians, Paul mentioned four things which Christians must surrender. He gave this assurance: God has special blessing for the one who surrenders. Listen!

1. SURRENDERING OUR RIGHTS
Philippians 4:1-7

"You, my Christian brothers, are my joy and reward because I won you for Christ," Paul wrote.

Show Illustration #13A

"I beg Euodias and Syntyche to be of the same mind in the Lord."

What a surprise that was to the Philippians! It was embarrassing enough to have Paul hear of the argument which divided the church. Now it was clear he even knew who had started it!

– 24 –

Show Illustration #6

The church members remembered what Paul had written earlier in the letter: "Have the same mind Christ had. He gave up His honor and glory. He stooped to become a servant. He humbled Himself and became obedient to the will of God even though it meant the death of the cross." (See 2:5-8.) Now he was saying that Euodias and Syntyche were to have that kind of mind: surrender their rights; give in to the other.

Paul commanded, "Rejoice in the Lord alway: and again I say, Rejoice." (See Philippians 4:4.)

The Philippians must have considered this carefully. One thought: These two women certainly haven't had any joy since the argument began. Another: The whole church had been affected by this situation. The matter would have to be settled so there could be joy.

The letter continued, "Let others see your gentleness, your yieldedness. Do not worry about anything. Pray about everything." (See Philippians 4:5-6.)

Euodias may have thought, *If I give in, if I surrender my rights, I'll be misunderstood. I'm not as wrong as Syntyche is.*

The Holy Spirit doubtless whispered, "Give in anyway. Don't care what others say. Never mind if all the blame is put on you. Do not be anxious. Don't worry about it. You may win the argument, you may insist on having your own way and yet lose all joy and peace."

Show Illustration #13

"If you will get this situation settled," Paul was saying, "the peace of God will guard your hearts."

2. SURRENDERING OUR THOUGHTS
Philippians 4:8-9

"All of you must have the right kinds of thoughts," Paul added. "Think of true things; of things that are right and pure and lovely. Think of things that are good. Think of things worth praising." (See Philippians 4:8; compare Proverbs 23:7.)

We are not told how the Philippians reacted. Nor do we know what the two women did. But maybe Syntyche decided, *Euodias has many good qualities. My thoughts of her have not all been right and pure. I've had a lot of unlovely thoughts. I'm going to ask her forgiveness.*

Show Illustration #14

If both women had forgiving thoughts, surely Syntyche turned to Euodias and Euodias turned to Syntyche. Each begged the other's forgiveness. Each confessed that her thoughts had been wrong. The others in the church agreed that from now on they all would let God control their thoughts. It was then that they heard Paul's words: "The God of peace shall be with you." (See Philippians 4:9.) The Philippians had the promise of double blessing: the peace of God guarding their hearts; the God of peace with them.

3. SURRENDERING OUR WILLS
Philippians 4:10-13

"I am full of joy," Paul added, "because you have taken such good care of me again."

For a long time–years perhaps–the Philippians had not known where Paul was. As soon as they had learned that he was in prison at Rome, they sent gifts to him. "I know you would have done this before if you could have. I did have needs, and you could have helped if you had known where I was. But I'm not complaining. I have learned to be content and happy with whatever I have. I know how to get along with almost nothing at all. I know how to live when I have much. I can do all things because Christ gives me strength."

The Philippians knew that it had been a long time since Paul had much in life to enjoy. Usually he had to get along with almost nothing. Sometimes he was hungry and thirsty and without clothes. He had no home of his own.

Show Illustration #15A

He preferred to spend all of his time doing missionary work and preaching. Instead, on occasion, he had to make tents to support himself.

Show Illustration #15B

He knew what it was to be beaten. Once he had been stoned and left for dead. (See 1 Corinthians 4:11-13.)

Show Illustration #15

And how many times he had been in prison! No matter where he was, Paul said, he was content. The Philippians understood why that was so. One day he had turned himself over to God. No longer would he follow his own will. He gave it up entirely. He chose to do God's will for the rest of his life. So when he was hungry and thirsty, God allowed it. His life was in God's hand whether he was preaching or making tents. If he was being stoned, God had hold of him. When he was in jail, it was because he had preached the Gospel. Surely God would not let go of him there. Since God was in control of his life, everything was all right. He was content. He could do all things and go through anything because Christ gave him strength.

4. SURRENDERING OUR MONEY
Philippians 4:14-23

The Philippians listened with pleasure as Paul continued to thank them for their gifts. "It is true that I have learned to be content in any situation. It is true that Christ gives me strength to go through anything. Even so, you showed your love by helping me in my present trouble. You also took care of my needs in the past, many times. Understand, I am not asking for gifts. However, I want you to have the rewards that God gives to those who share."

Show Illustration #16A

"Right now, since Epaphroditus brought your gifts, I have everything I need, even more than I need!" Paul continued, "What you have sent is a sweet-smelling sacrifice which pleases God."

The Philippians would have understood that. Long before their time God had instructed His people to offer certain sacrifices to Him. One was the burnt offering sacrifice. (See Leviticus 1:1-17.)

Show Illustration #16b

This was a sacrifice which the worshiper could give "of his own voluntary will" (Leviticus 1:3). He brought either an animal or a bird which was burned on the altar. It is spoken of as a "sweet-savour offering," a sweet-smelling sacrifice. God is pleased when His people give themselves willingly to Him. So the Philippians understood that Paul was saying that their gift to him was a burnt sacrifice to God. It showed they had willingly surrendered themselves to Him. Because it smelled sweet to God, it was a sacrifice which God accepted with pleasure.

Do you think the Philippians had joy when they heard that? Imagine how they felt when Paul added, "But my God shall supply everything you need according to His riches in glory by Christ Jesus." (See Philippians 4:19.) Think of that! They'd given themselves to God. They'd given their money to God's servant. Consequently, God would supply everything they needed.

Perhaps the Philippians wondered how this could be true. If so, God could have reminded them of this: Once, the Lord Jesus borrowed Simon Peter's fishing boat. He sat in it, teaching the people who lined the seashore. After the meeting was over and the sermon was finished, He said to Peter, "Go out in the deep water and put down your nets for some fish." Peter thought it was foolish, for he had fished all night without catching a thing. He knew that if the fish did not bite at night, they would not bite in the bright sunlight. However, he grudgingly obeyed. As a result, he caught so many fish that the boat began to sink. Simon Peter had lent his boat to Jesus. The Lord filled it with fish to make up for the night in which he had caught nothing. (See Luke 5:1-11.)

Just so, God supplies the needs of those who share with His servants.

Paul's letter, although written long ago to the Philippians, is also for us today. God has kept it in His Word so that we will learn from it.

Are you the kind of person who insists on your rights? Perhaps you and another Christian have disagreed. The matter has not been settled because you have insisted on having your own way. If so, now is the time to do something about it. Ask the Lord's forgiveness. Tell Him you are willing to surrender your rights. Promise Him that you will make it right with your friend today, or as soon as you possibly can. Then you will have His peace to guard your heart.

What about your thoughts? Do you think loving, kind, pure things? If not, ask God to forgive you. Surrender your thinking habits to Him. If you will let Him control your thoughts, you can be certain of this: the God of peace shall be with you.

Have you turned your will over to God? Are you letting Him control your life completely? If not, will you do so right now? Then you will know what it means to be perfectly content. No matter what happens, you will know that God has allowed it. Because He has permitted it, He will give you strength to endure it.

What about your money? You know that everything comes from the Lord. Have you been sharing what you have with those who are His servants? If you are willing to do this, God will help you. Then you will experience the joy of having Him supply all your needs.

Once all these matters are settled, you will "rejoice in the Lord always." For there really is joy in surrender.

www.ingramcontent.com/pod-product-compliance
Lightning Source LLC
Chambersburg PA
CBHW060803090426
42736CB00002B/137